To Fret or not to Fret

Prayers to lead you and
challenge you, if you want…

Grant Everson

Not just another book of prayer

This is not just another book of prayers but,
You can use it as that, stand alone prayers when you
need the words to express your deepest emotions.

These prayers are also meant to encourage you
To use them as a "diving board", start with a prayer
But add, make it your own.
Add names, places, add emotions, feelings
Draw, doodle, use colours that bring out the emotive
Part of the prayer that you feel

For prayer is poetry, and yet creativity, and yet
Our deepest longing and emotion
Our cries to God,
Our hope that the God of the Universe hears us
Our praise, our thanks
So use this little book of prayers to challenge
And inspire you.

My special thanks to the people who have inspired me:

Audrey and Zoe, Mum Marlene and Dad Cyril

And for those who have prayed, encouraged and contributed especially:
Candice Williams, Rev Sharon Davis, Patrick Jordi and Samantha Naldrett

Forward

Much of our praying is often necessitated by a crisis of some sort. Family, work, relationships, future, decisions, purchases, illness, death, new life, and the list grows rather than shrinks. Any reason to pray is a good reason to pray, there's no right or wrong reason, there's no right or wrong way to pray. But the more we pray the better we get at it. What do I mean by that? Well, praying does seem to have a language all of its own. The more we pray the more we increase our praying vocabulary.

When I worked for a Christian organisation we prayed as a staff every morning. I was quite intimidated by these more mature staff members who seemed to have all the right words for all the right prayers. So you can guess I was a rather silent prayer buddy during these times. But one of these more mature staff encouraged me to pray out loud as it didn't matter what I prayed, everyone would then know what was on my heart, which was more important.

I thought that a gentle way of encouraging me and as I became bold, so more words were added to my public praying vocabulary.

We also get better at not rushing in and out of prayer but discover that taking time to pray becomes easier and not a chore. At the heart of our prayer journey is our relationship with the Father, the conversation we're trying to have with Him, the words we're using, the vocabulary we're growing and using. And time means we not only get to speak words but we start to learn and become comfortable with listening and being quiet. Prayer equals a relationship with the father. A relationship equals speaking and listening.

Does praying actually work, or should I rather ask, "Does it make a difference?" Is it just "pie in the sky"? Every religion has an action of prayer or prayer format. Believers and non-believers the world over all turn to praying at some point in their lives, recognising that even behind the bravado of "relying on myself", there comes a time when "myself" doesn't hold all the keys. We sometimes pray at God but we need to be encouraged to pray with God, having a conversation with Him and not AT Him. I'm not trying to invent a prayer system with this publication, I'm mindful of the plethora of helpful books on why we should pray and helpful on how to pray and the many electronic applications that give us helpful prayers for every occasion.

Crucial to us choosing to pray is the recognition that we don't hold all the "keys" and turning to God is a very natural response. Trusting God with our stuff is very personal, whether we keep a prayer journal or just pray in our heads. And we can't negate the feeling we experience when we pray, and yes, it's not about feelings, but we do have a response that is internal when we come to pray and that is just as important as it's our spirit finding a connection, you might say.

We pray as a last response, that is true, but we also pray as a natural course of action, a natural trusting in God that is akin to a partnership. Some may say that praying comes quite naturally and easily, others might say it's not that easy, in fact sometimes it's quite a hard slog getting round to making the time to pray then actually having to be still and pray words.

My hope is that you are enthused as you use the prayers I have gathered. The prayers are sectioned or categorised, but we know that as we sit and think as we pray, our thoughts often run havoc in our heads and we can pray "all around the world". I want to encourage that, speak out the things that fill your mind, God wants to hear all that. The categories are meant to be a help not a hindrance.

As much as the prayers are set having a focus, the intention is that you will be able to use them over and over in their format, but I also want them to act as "diving boards", a place from which to launch into further prayer, to add your own lyrics. To create new splashes as you "break water" for the first time. You can make these prayers as simple or as challenging as you like.

GE, April 2020

A Life Without God (Introduction)

Some choose a life without God, some chose a life with God as central to all their decision-making, work, life, relationships,
worship. The one thing we do know is that many chose to pray, whether they are believers or not, because they understand that the world is bigger than we can sometimes explain. Some see God in the little things around them, some discard the little things, some see the little things as being the result of a created work and order.

In this first section you have an opportunity to explore some of the thoughts prevalent about a life "Without God" and maybe you are challenged to look a bit deeper, think a bit deeper, and wonder a bit deeper.

A life without God..

A life without God, putting all our energy into work and pastimes to fill the empty hours.
Shouting support as followers of our favourite sporting teams or Celebs whose lives we aspire to emulate.
Having endless conversations about overpaid footballers and nouveau Celebs as if they have a direct impact on our lives, but they don't really care about us.

Pursuing relationships and friendships that make us feel good about ourselves, we take and take and take to fulfill our own mission.
Social media is our god, we are the centre of the universe
We connect ourselves to the lives of others we see through Reality tv.

Therein lie the anomaly, is it really reality?
Whose reality?

A Life Without God

Choosing a spirituality that focuses on me
A spirituality that brings me peace as I strive to attain
A level of calm, ultimately blocking out the World
Putting faith in inanimate objects
Believing that more faith earns us more points
As we climb the ladder of spiritual hierarchy.
Believing in ideologies dreamt up by man
Without a good critique of the source
Our personal reality trumps anything that might be bigger,
And outside of ourselves.
Prayers are for the weak who need a crutch

My spirituality is personal,
I shape it around my needs
My spirituality is personal,
I need it to calm me
My spirituality is personal,
I can turn to it when I need to
My spirituality is personal,
it's my "go to" medication

A Life Without God

If there was a God the world would be without all its
chaos
If there was a God why didn't my child find healing
through all Our prayers
And what about the Holocaust?
What about children in poverty?
And what about pandemics?

I went to church, it was all about old hymns
The leader was dressed in a uniform that seemed to
come from a wardrobe of the Middle Ages
He didn't grab my attention and anyway
I came to see God

Why so many religions?
How do I know which one to believe or trust?
Prayers seem like endless one way traffic,
When I do engage with them.

If there was a God surely we would only need one
church
All believing the same thing because
He would tell us what to believe

I went to church, it was all about rock music and lights
The leader was dressed in a uniform that seemed to
come from a top end high street shop

He shouted at me, he didn't grab my attention
Anyway I came to see God

Why so many courses to find God
How do I know which one to believe or trust
Prayers still seem like endless one way traffic
When I try to engage with them.

A Life Without God

Today I saw a bird building a nest and wondered
What the bird was thinking or how it even worked
Out the design process.
I saw a spider weaving a silky web
Pure Artistry, by design, a trap.
Who taught the spider such art and patience.
In the garden I saw the prettiest weeds
Even the weeds have a role in the biological system
But such thorny stems to keep us away.

Don't you hate those creeping weed-like phenomenon
They wind their way around anything that doesn't
move
Other plants, the garden furniture, the garden fence
How clever, when you think about it.

Today I saw a dog herding a toddler in the park
What's that about?
What was the dog thinking, surely it knows the
difference,
Between a human and an animal
Pure instinct perhaps.

A life Without God

Fast food, not so fast food
Fancy names for machine produced versions of coffee
Food menus that provide more promise than the
actual culinary delights
A feast of world delights all in the same square
A global experience without having to leave our
borders
Dining becomes our taste of heaven

Why can't we pick our kind of god from a machine
There can be different kinds and specials on particular
days
It's easier to pay for something we want than to
Spend ages making it at home
Maybe the three for £10 experience
And if God were in a machine we'd know exactly
What we're getting for our money
And can always get a refund if we don't like the
experience.
Shopping for our kind of god.

TV, the Internet, all offer us this brand of God we can consume
From the comfort of our homes.
We can change the channels
If we don't like what is served to us.
We can just swipe left or right whatever is correct
And what about all those other religions,

We need more variety for our shopping basket
Maybe we can just "like" them, surely that means something.

A life Without God

The bustling city, commuters, visitors, aliens
All with a mission, some to earn, some to explore,
Some to taste the sites, some to feel safe and safe
All with a purpose of achieving a personal goal

Many faces, Faces masking a life
A life made wealthy due to hard work
A life concealing the pain of home
A life riddled with questions of self worth
A life too afraid to change the circumstances
Many faces, many masks

People wearing masks
Making a statement about the environment
Making a statement about the smells
Making a statement about belief systems

Many noises
Friends excitedly sharing experiences
People on their mobile phones in their own little worlds
Workers moving, carrying things
Cranes to help with the really big things
Vans stopping and starting, delivering things.
Siren, always sirens.

At the start of the day with Candice Williams

Dear Father,

As I start this day, thankful for all I have received from Your Hand,
I pray for your mercy and blessing, Father.
That I, and those I love, will be safe and well on the paths we travel;
That I will be patient with those who cross my way;
That I will forgive when I feel slighted or hurt and also, that I will be kind to those in need.
I pray, Father, that I will seek Your Will in all I do and that I will be a testament to your love.
Amen

Dear Lord,

Sometimes we forget to seek Your Face
and listen to your promises,
Especially when life is busy and seems overwhelming.
May this day be different, Lord.
I pray that I may quiet the noise of the world
and the angst of my heart and mind and just rest in
you.
Listening, with a yearning heart, for your comfort and
Direction.
Above all else Lord,
I pray that I will not be scared to follow where you are
leading
And that I will trust in you and the promises of your
word.

Amen

A NEW DAY

Morning Lord!!!

A new day of new promises, new miracles
New smells, new tastes and most of all,
New Life
Yesterday is gone forever, like starting the clock again
Not in a "groundhog" sort of day, but a blank canvass,
Kind of day

Open my eyes to the opportunities of today, Lord
Open my arms to the challenges that will make today,
Richer than yesterday
Open my heart to receive goodness but also to lavish,
Goodness on people who will be in special need
today.

Amen

A Prayer for your Presence, O My God

Lord God, your presence is everywhere, Yet my eyes are blinded to see You

Teach me to see you with my whole life

Each, and every day, may my heart longs to take delight in all that is around me .

May I awaken to the new day dawning with quiet expectation anticipating the joy of all that will unfold The gift of your mercy as I step onto the threshold of the adventure of this day.

May I be open and willing to listen to the silence and hear your voice

To be still, not rushing ahead or running too far down the path.

May I be brave enough to hold uncertainty and embrace the unknown that I might grow to know something has already begun

And I may participate in the work of your love

Amen

Rev Sharon Davis

CONFESSION

Forgive us our sins as we forgive others' who sin against us

Father I pray the truth of that statement, that you would Forgive me.
Forgive me today for my behaviour, Forgive me.
For my Words that may have caused distress
Forgive me for my actions that might have seemed stupid or cynical.

Lord as I am still, reflecting on today, remind me of some things
That have infuriated others about me
Words that have carried the weight of a dagger to innocent hearts.
Words and actions that have not shown me to be a witness for You.

Holy Spirit pour into my heart your cleansing power, wash out the grime, both intentional and unintentional
All those impurities that clog up everything
Make me clean again Lord!!

Forgive me Father and help me to forgive others

"To Church or not to Church?"
What a question!!

I always remember walking past the big dark church on our street. By day just another ordinary building but at night it seemed to take on a different personality. It was dark and almost terrifying to me as a young boy, and I was often too afraid to look at it for fear of being captured and taken into its darkness. What a silly thought now when our view of church buildings is that of a sanctuary, a place of respite. It's also a place of community where people get together and find out about life and love.

I suppose, mostly we associate a church building with the opportunity to sing songs of worship and be taught the old biblical themes and stories. In our modern contexts the building serves young people's groups and coffee mornings and possibly community music venues. So much power attached to a building.

But we do have an affinity with Temple worship and our church buildings today stand in the place of the Temple of old. And the Temple had a space for community worship of God. And the Temple had a "Holy Place" where God resided. The Temple was the place to visit and worship God.

We do know that we are able to worship God outside of the confines of a building space. The Temple is within us, because God lives within us. So our worship and praise of Him is "sans frontieres". Where we go, He goes, which means where we go with Him is always Holy Ground.

So let's not be afraid to plant our feet on the ground and speak words of worship, words of praise, words of adoration. We have no church walls to measure space and measure our
adoration. How freeing is that? To think that as much as we have an affinity to Temple worship, we are now portable Temples, taking God with us wherever we go.

PRAISE SONG

Lord my heart is full of love and joy and other feelings I
don't have words for
Thank you Lord for giving me life, giving me family and
giving me
Special people to love and share love with.
When I look back and see how you have loved me,
how you have coloured my life,
I know it's a treat You lavish on me.
Nothing I do in my own strength gives me pleasure as
much as when you order things in my life, I believe.
I praise you Lord because you made me and know me
and you know the things that make my heart sing.
Lord you also know what causes me distress and
saddens my heart
You know the things I find easy in life but also the
things that I would describe as hard or difficult in my
life
But your love for me is constant, I believe that, as you
Continue to be with me on this journey.

So Father I add my praise to the many words and
songs
That have been sung and said before.
You are the God of the universe, and also the God of
my life.

Amen

TATTY PRAISE

Lord of all creation, of the water, sea and sky, of
planets known and unknown
Our praise and worship of you comes easily
sometimes
When life is full and busy with the things we love.
Praise is easy when our hearts are easily joyful
because there are no obstacles to distract us.
Weather, family, work, friends are some of the things
that cause our hearts to sing
But when we have to negotiate obstacles every day,
our worship of you can be a bit tatty, almost
non-existent.
In the tatty times, O Lord, I also want to honour your
name

When all I can see are obstacles
I want to have xray eyes to see through the obstacles
And sing a song of worship to you.
We are a generation always wanting a sign,
Something to focus our attention on that gives us
heart.
May our sign be the reminder that you are the Lord of
all Creation.

My Father, accept my worship of you
Accept the words that struggle to express my worship
As I am negotiating obstacles
Father accept my praise when it's not as colourful
As when things seem perfect.
I want to praise you when it's stormy and tatty
Father help me to open my heart to you
So that my response to you comes from a place that wants,
Wants to worship you and recognise your love for me,
In the good times and the routh times, Lord.
I praise you.

Praise Maketh Me

Lord Jesus, I want my life to declare the glory of
your name.
I want my life to recognise you as the God to be
praised.

Praise you when the sun is burning on my face
Praise you when the wind is bending the trees
Praise you in the centre of the chaos in my life
Praise you in the still and quiet time that feels
Like a lonely place
Praise you when I don't feel like praising you
Praise you when I am excited about tomorrow
Praise you when I'm afraid of what tomorrow
Might bring
Praise you when sorrow overcomes me
When I think of family and friends in distress
Praise you when others are filled with joy
For your blessings

Praise you when my cupboard is bare
Praise you when my fridge can't hold the shopping
Praise you for my intellect
Praise you when I'm clueless

Praise you when I feel loved
Praise you when love hurts

May my life recognise you, Lord,
As the God to be praised.
Amen.

You Love Me

Lord your love never runs out on me, it's higher

and wider than I can ever know or imagine

People have written about your love, sung songs

about your love, about our experience of your love

When I fall into the depths of feeling hurt, despondent
or broken,

You still love me. I believe that as an act of my faith in
you.

When I feel like I'm riding on a cloud, ecstatic and wild
with joy. You love me.

Your Word says you knew me before I was born

When I was still in the watery place of unbirth.

You loved me then while I was being formed.

In my own times of feeling lost and alone

Lord you still love me.

I'm never sure Lord, when, when I first realised

the enormity of your love.

But I understand what a constant Father you are
whose pleasure is always to love me

Your love is a marker for my life.

**Words from Psalm 139
The Bible**

Thank you

Father, thank you.
You don't turn a deaf ear when I lament
You put up with my daily, boring, cry for your help
Thank you, Father.

I ask, or cry about the things that will be my daily
portion you provide, and I realise my expectation is
different.
And often don't recognise the form of your blessing.
Father, thank you.

Protection and provision is my daily need
Just like the Israelites in the desert
You didn't fail them and you never fail me
Help me to recognise my true need each day.
Thank you, Father.

Lord each day you fill my life
With food, warmth, protection, and a
Whole host of things I don't even ask for
Thank you Lord.

Faraway God

Travel is so easy nowadays with access to most destinations. Even places that we once described as "remote" we are now able to access because we are clever at problem solving. Engineering and aviation have made our world a smaller place, but the biggest feat must be the probes we've been able to send into space bringing us knowledge of some of the planets we might count as neighbours.

As a child I was led to believe that God resided in those far reaching places up in the sky possibly among the stars. And travel to those stars would take years, but in a strange way, God could see us but we couldn't see Him. Should we blame our parents for misleading us or trying to metaphorically describe the distance we believed God to be in relation to us?

Sometimes as adults we buy into that picture, or console ourselves with the fact that God resides somewhere far away and is inaccessible. Young people, so accustomed to our "MacDonalds" culture, may also demand instant or "on tap" favour from God.

Distance and silence is painted in the same framework, we don't hear from God, He is far away from us.

Is God ever silent? Or do we want His communication to be on our terms, in our language, our picture format.

What a Calling

If one of the priorities of finding the right job is about stability, maybe it's time to focus more on purpose and calling and "all these things shall be added unto you".

Lord just grab me by the shoulders and turn me to face the direction you want me to face

Ilove praying but I do feel despondent sometimes when I feel as though I'm praying into a vacuum,   I feel as though I have the faith but my life experience is less when compared to others in similar circumstances, I feel so hopeless.

Father I want to serve you completely serve you in my family and place of work

And want to know that you can and will use me completely
I don't want to feel useless, that I'm letting you down,
We all have different callings in life I know
Lord would you nudge me in the direction, closer to the people you want me to impact

Help my focus to move away from the benefits or rewards of my job and to rather see the role I can play with fellow colleagues, friends and family.

Amen.

Are we there yet

Lord of mercy, Lord of grace
Help me find my way on this rocky road.
Help me.

The world is so divided, and the divisions
They bring so much pain
On the bus in the morning,
On the train in the evening
I can see so much isolation,
I can feel the pain
I can feel the contortions of my own spirit
At each and every station, there are exits and
entrances

Often there's a massive push through the doors
As the world comes crowding in
Pushing in.
Crushing forward.
Infiltrating space.
Lord help me find your sanctuary;
The world is always pushing in.

Lord make a Believer of me yet
Enfold me and embrace me like a long lost son
A child who longs for lost love
A child standing isolated and alone on the station
platform midst the crazy rush
The coming and the going of frenzied trains.

Lord, if you are the driver
Tell me what is our destination
In a child's voice I want to ask,
"Are we there yet?"

Patrick Jordi

The Steering Wheel

Father God we believe that you know all things.
You know where we come from and where we
are going. Sometimes I just want you to show me a
map or satellite image of the destination for me.
And to take away the angst of not knowing what to do
or where to go.

Father God give me the wisdom and an ear to hear
and understand your guiding hand in and over my life,
give me patience to trust because I can't see the
whole picture you are drawing.
Lord close the doors you don't want me to walk
through, turn on the light to illuminate the path you
want me to follow.

Father give me the heart of an explorer
The courage to step where I haven't stepped before
Discovery is gained by putting one foot ahead of the
other
Turning thoughts and feelings into action
More courage, I pray Father.
To trust what I hear you saying.
Onward.

Amen.

A prayer for guidance

Father God

Thank You that you love me more than
I can imagine
And that You have destined me for great things.

Please show me what these things are and cover
me with Your peace
While I wait for You to reveal them to me,
in Your time.

Please also bless me with discernment and a
Willing spirit to recognise my God-given opportunities
And follow, bravely, the paths You have set for me.

Help me to remember that You are in control and that I
don't need to worry about the unknown because
You, Lord, are guiding me.

Amen

Samantha Naldrett

*Be still, stay with the things you want guidance for
Boldly offer them to God, name them.*

*What paths or opportunities does the Lord seem
to be showing you?*
*Make a commitment to explore one of them in the
next 24 hours*

BE MY PROVIDER

Lord, the world seems closing in on me
I feel hemmed in on every side
My mind creates enemies all around me
I get anxious trying to make decisions.
Even little ones, insignificant ones.
I feel as though I'm having to fight my way through
A sea of people travelling in the opposite direction
It's relentless, one situation after another
It feels like chaos, a runaway roller coaster
No stopping, just more momentum I cannot control
Lord I want to breathe……

Release me from this knot I feel inside that seems to,
grip tighter and tighter
Holy Spirit come and break these chains I cannot see
Chains that seem to bind my head and thoughts
Holy Spirit, release me from these feelings that make
me feel less than who I am.

Father God I pray for your Spirit to abide in me
Bring me peace, bring me an inward smile
Give me courage to push against the walls that
Seem to hem me in and create self doubt.

Lord you know me and know my deepest thoughts
Please help me to banish those thoughts
Thoughts that make me feel less of myself.
Into your hands I place my thoughts, my decisions
The things that make me anxious
Lord give me courage to take control.
And wisdom to respond.

Amen.

Maybe take some time to name the thoughts and write them down if you can be honest enough with yourself. It's private just you and God.

Lost Ones

We always lose friends, and sometimes, family through all kinds of circumstances or situations. They move or we move, we lose contact sometimes without reason. We write it off and accept and say, "that's life". We cope because we have a chain or friends and we know it's not a permanent loss. We don't negate the years of conversation and being in each other's lives. They have been the building blocks of our friendships. We are saddened by the separation of distance, but have a knowledge that it will be a relationship that will always exist.

But when we lose forever, we are confronted by different emotions, sometimes emotions that we've never encountered before. Confronted by the permanence of losing relationships forever, is a shock to our system.

We deeply accept, I think, that news will come suddenly one day of searing loss. But we are never prepared for the news, the reality.

Today, this moment in time, (April 2020) we are confronted by a virus much like we'd see in a film. Scary, apocalyptic, world-wide, no vaccine, medical services stretched. A world-wide phenomenon, something we all bear the cost of. Maybe just as scary as war, but an unseen enemy.

And we don't know how to pray at this point in time. The right words fail us, or don't even seem to exist.

GONE

For the times we lose those close to us but don't know what to pray.

Lord Jesus my heart is saddened, almost broken
I am numb to this feeling of loss, I don't know how to
describe it.
A hole inside of me, dark, black, a hole.
Nobody can see how big or dark and scary it is.
All I know, is that it feels so empty, so empty, so very
empty. How? Why?
And the words that people offer as comfort I hear but
don't really hear
As I'm confused and angry and sad all at the same
time.

I don't have words
I have feelings and thoughts and questions
I don't have words
I want it to be yesterday when it was different and
okay
I don't have words.

I want to curl up somewhere away from the noise and talking.

Lord Jesus be the comforter, for me and others
You don't need to say anything Lord Jesus,
I just need to know you are here
You don't need to understand my pain
I just need to know you are here

The memories of lost ones are often just as strong as the prayers we try and console ourselves with. It's okay if you can't find the words, the memories are just as powerful.

And symbols such as lighting a candle, or many candles, sometimes stand instead of the words we don't have, or the feelings we can't describe.

Light a candle today….

At the end of the Day

All is quiet, a sure sign the day is winding down. Thinking over the day will bring a smile or grin to your face, frustration or a giggle as you recall an event, moment or a comment made by someone you overheard. Your body is also in relaxed mode, ready to just give and allow sleep to wash over you.

But before that happens, you're still mentally sifting through some things, making plans for tomorrow, thinking of things you can put on your list that needs sorting out, people to call or message. It's as if the day never ends. We start the day on our phones and finish the day on our phones, checking those last minute possible messages or social media posts.

This is slowing down time, late night coffee time, reading a few lines from that book you're trying to get through time even though it doesn't seem to make sense or stick in your memory. Best of all, it's you just you and your thoughts. Dreams about the future, and thinking about the reality of today. Family and friends, maybe saying a prayer for them as you remember one needing a prayer. For their health, for another a difficult work situation, another, kids struggling with school, the list is always there for you to give attention to. And as you think about them you are drawn again into the relationship you share with them. They say you can't choose family, and maybe it's not such a bad idea that we have no choice, haha.

We've almost stopped, just a few more things to process before we can finally say goodbye to the day. Did you stop to smell the roses today or was it just another frantic rush? Even watching TV in the evening can seem like a rush trying to get settled in time for the film or documentary or sitcom. Breathe out, breathe out the "rubbish" of the day. Breathe in, breathe in the sweet fragrances of the day. Just breathe.

At the end of the Day

Lord, it's quiet, the end of the day, all things are done,
well basically.
Bed is such a nice thought and it's calling my name
Thank you for this day with it's laughter and
challenging moments
I'm sorry if I missed opportunities today to say a kind
word or share a hug
With someone who needed to be noticed.
Give me another opportunity tomorrow, please.

Thank you that I have a bed and a safe place to sleep
I pray for the many who tonight will be sleeping rough
and having to cope with the weather and trying to stay
safe.

Father be their guardian angel, their protector.
And as I contemplate the day, I pray that you will give
me complete rest so that my body will be renewed.

Amen

At the end of the day

Unpacking the dishwasher
Each clean dish has its own story of service today
Wiping the last droplets before placing cups, plates,
glasses,
In their rightful place.

Unpacking the dishwasher can be quite robotic
No thought or concentration needed
But an opportunity to let the mind wander and reflect
on the day,
Missed opportunities come to mind
Moments that bring a smile or quiet chuckle
A tinge of sadness remembering someone in distress
Or feeling sadness remembering the loss of someone
close.

Father, thank you for helping me see the day in
perspective
For helping me realise my participation in people's
Lives is both active and non
At the end of the day I see a little more clearly
A little more clearly of what you're about Lord
A little more clearly of your love coming down.

At the end of the day the house settles down
With all it's quirky noises
At the end of the day I hear you more clearly
As the quirky noises in my head settle and finds rest.

Lord Jesus, as I slow down at the end of the day
May you please bring peace to my beating heart

Amen

Of Illness and operations

Father God, you are the healer of all illness
The surgeon of all operations, for you know us and
created us.
All of your creation is perfect because we bare
your seal, the mark of your creative spirit

Our bodies are subject to the way we treat it and
susceptible to all illness
We have no control
Lord we need your healing miracle when life
throws illness over us and is
Too great for our medicines

Be the healer who guides the surgeon who cuts
into the body
To remove that tumor doing so much damage and
causing so much angst
I pray wisdom on the surgical teams as they make
decisions and deliver their expert care.

As they deliver expert care to make life richer.

Amen

We don't sometimes know how to pray for important operations
We pray lots of words in our confusion
Be bold to name the reason or illness
Recognise the skilled people God is using
Boldly pray for God's will to be done

THE CLIMATE

Lord you created all things by speaking this world into being
You give us the ability to master and care for this creative space you placed us on
Our greed and selfishness has led us to being more masters than carers of this world, significantly changing things that affect us daily.

We talk about our carbon footprint, we are aghast at the melting ice caps, we blame others for the erosion of helpless animals for trophy and industry
Our waste is the symptom of the "Macdonalds" culture we have created
Poverty and ill-health are exacerbated by us plundering the planet, plastic, glass, metal, pollution, water, fire, temperatures.

Things we talk about as if we're just spectators
Lord give us back a love for your planet
Remind us Lord that you saw all that had been created and you described it as being
"Good"
Lord we want to see and experience our world as Good

We pray for nations to take seriously the knowledge that

Our Planet is in desperate need of saving from the changes to its climate,
Give us courage to participate in an option that changes our own Environment
Challenge me to recycle, challenge me to spend ethically,
Challenge me to become an ambassador for the good of our World.

Amen

**Words from Genesis 1
The Bible**

OUR WORLD

God bless our world
Guide our leaders
Give voice to the environmentalists
Courage to cut carbon emissions
Wisdom to replace plastic packaging
More planting of trees

God bless our world
Land animals and the fish of the sea
Give voice to climate change Ambassadors
Courage to cut waste
Wisdom to purchase ethically
And a pride for our home

God bless our world
Plants, veggies and the fight against pesticides
The birds of the air as they feed
The changing habitats of little animals
Wisdom to tend the soil
And a pride for our home.

Amen

A WORLD IN CHAINS

Is the world nearing its end, O lord of all creation?
The world doesn't look familiar anymore
People don't seem to need interact
We don't use banks
We don't need to push trolleys in the supermarket
either
Our phones have screens and cameras

Lord we have not been slow to use the gifts and skills
you've given us.
To advance the world because you give us wisdom
and the creativity and authority

Father I pray that in an era of so much self-indulgence
And so much belief in the individual being number
one,
That we start to look more intently at the world around
us
That we have an awareness or "awokeness"
Of things that are less about ourselves and more
about other people and nations
Realising that sometimes what we think we need
Pales into insignificance when seeing the needs
Of our neighbours and those different to us.
Father give us a new vision,
A new revelation for your world and your people
May we have your heart in the way it transcends
technology

May we be about love and serving others

Father, we need to interact, we need to break the
chains of isolation
And of mental ill-health.
Father help us to push trolleys again
To say hello to neighbours
To not make life all about,
Our phones with their screens and cameras.

Amen

HOME

Father thank you for the safety and security of home
More than just a physical place in which we live
But a space we make our own, temporary or
permanent
Thank you Lord that home means a space in which to
be ourselves,
Put up our pictures, and quirky mugs
For copious amounts of coffee and tea.
Thank you Lord that home allows us a personal
expression,
Of individuality and family which allows us to invite
others into the space to share our lives.

Thank you that home allows us a space to curl up
And hide from the world when we desperately need
sanctuary and our own chapel with you.

Flowers, candles, herbs, the fragrances that perfume
our home like a comfort blanket
Music and colours and light that create, not just, an
ambience.
But a place of warmth.

Thank you Lord that Home is also a power pack that energises us to take on the world
We are filled up, we are re-charged, we are educated.
We are excited, we are then like straight arrows
Directed and sent out

Lord thank you for home that goes where we go in our hearts.

Amen.

Grant F Everson was born and grew up Cape Town, South Africa during the Apartheid era. Growing in faith meant balancing politics, ethics and practically what it meant to follow Jesus. Mixing faith and politics didn't mix, apparently, but they both played a role in the formation of many people's lives, navigating the world trying to find their place and following the call to follow Jesus in a divided society. A call to Christian ministry resulted in the privilege of being involved in youth and community ministry for more than 25 years, both in South Africa and the United Kingdom. A keen sportsperson, thinker and practical theologian, this is his first published work.